J. CAMPBELL CHILDERHOSE

As an Intervenor and Teacher of the Deafblind, I became aware of the need in children's libraries, for a personal history of Canada. With appreciation, I dedicate this book to my long-time student Jason Hotte, and to my husband Ted Childerhose, both of whom, love Canada as much as I.

J. Campbell Childerhose

Order this book online at www.trafford.com
or email orders@trafford.com

Most Trafford titles are also available at major online book retailers.

 **Trafford** PUBLISHING® www.trafford.com

North America & international
toll-free: 844 688 6899 (USA & Canada)
fax: 812 355 4082

Our mission is to efficiently provide the world's finest, most comprehensive book publishing service, enabling every author to experience success. To find out how to publish your book, your way, and have it available worldwide, visit us online at www.trafford.com

Because of the dynamic nature of the Internet, any web addresses or links contained in this book may have changed since publication and may no longer be valid. The views expressed in this work are solely those of the author and do not necessarily reflect the views of the publisher, and the publisher hereby disclaims any responsibility for them.

ISBN: 978-1-4120-5986-2 (sc)
ISBN: 978-1-4669-8152-2 (e)

Print information available on the last page.

Trafford rev. 02/26/2021

FORWARD

Like my cousin Donald, and uncles Alexander, Wilford, Joe, Gil and Romeo, I am nurturing a military spirit. My husband Edward George (Ted) who was named in the tradition of the royal family by his mother Ethel, has been in the Canadian Air Force for 27 years. Once informed that our next posting would lead us to Colorado, I began to dig through boxes that I seem only to open, when I'm being uprooted. However, unlike Donald, Alexander and Wilford who during both World Wars were buried at sea or in Europe, I would be going home after four years.

In a box that contained the oldest of my possessions, I found with a figure skating program from March 1967, my Centennial Athlete badge, a commemorative Confederation dollar, as well as pictures and postcards from Expo 67. As was my grandmother Rita Green, my paternal grandmother Florence Campbell, was a retired teacher who insisted on saving all these mementos. She also gave my sister Donna and I diaries, emphasizing that Canada's 100th Birthday would be a once-in-a-lifetime experience. Both were lost in the many moves of life, but using these souvenirs, I have been able to recreate one of the happiest times in my childhood!

Through Grandma Florence's stories of family members, she showed me that though separated by years, death or experiences, we were still connected by one root. I came to know them, in association with historical events or the lives of historical figures. In the weekends spent with Grandma, I realized her love of history was interwoven with her love of family. I recall her explaining in the 1960's, the crocheted patterns she had created, to record the Apollo space missions, in tablecloths for her children. With Grandma's history-happens-at-home approach, I often wonder how she would have celebrated the entrance of Nunavut, into Canadian Confederation! Often a writer of poetry, Grandma may have written the following:

Nunavut

In 99', Robert told me how to remember the third territory,

Joining Confederation 50 years after Newfoundland, the rest of Canada's story.

He said, "We can have all of it, or we can have none of it."

So now, Canadians have, their newest, northerly, Nunavut!

By J. Campbell Childerhose

<u>**January 1967**</u>

Dear Diary,

It's January again, and we're starting a *wh-o-o-o-o-le, n-ew-ew-ew-ew,*  year full of holidays and fun times, with our families and friends. Mr. P., my Grade 4 teacher, said that 1967 is going to be "Th-ee-ee-ee-ee Y-ee-ee-ee-ee-ar of the Cen-n-n-n-tur-r-r-r-ry-y-y-y-y"! This is the year, that we'll all turn 100 years old, so we're all invited to the BIGGEST PARTY that Canada has ever had!

Grandma Campbell gave my sister Donna and I, diaries for Christmas, so that *o-o-o-o-ne, da-a-a-a-y,* our kids will be able to read, *a-a-a-a-ll* about Canada's Centennial Year. "Centennial" means 100. One thing our city is doing is building a new high school and it's going to be called Centennial Secondary School.

Grandma told me that while I was sleeping at midnight on January 1st 1967, our Prime Minister Lester B. Pearson, started off the party by lighting the new Centennial Flame. It has the shields that represent the 10 Canadian Provinces and 2 territories making a circle like a Christmas wreath, around it. They're all made out of cement and are sitting in a fountain. That way *n-n-n-n--o-o-o-o-thing,* can catch on fire. Prime Minister Pearson gets to see it everyday because it's in front of the Parliament Buildings where he works in Ottawa, Ontario, the capital city of Canada.

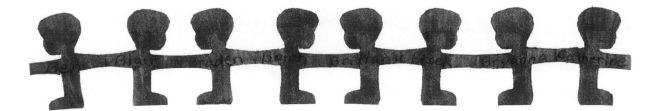

CANADIAN CONFEDERATION JULY 1st 1867

Sir John A. Macdonald and the Confederation Fathers

PRIME MINISTER PEARSON LIGHTS CENTENNIAL FLAME

CONFÉDÉRATION CANADIENNE

The Centennial Flame will help Canadians remember when Canada first became a country on July 1st 1867. That was the day, when we got our first Prime Minister. His name was Sir John A. Macdonald. He wasn't always called "Sir". Before this, he used to be called "Mr.". Then Queen Victoria made him into a knight because it took a *r-e-e-e-ally* brave person, to get *a-a-a-all* the people living in the Canadian colonies to agree on anything!

The French people couldn't forget that they were the first European people to move to Canada. After that, the British people moved here when they won a war against the French people. Then, everyone *ki-i-i-i-nd of f-f-f-for-or-or-or-go-o-o-o-t*, that the North American Indian people were already living here, so it was their country first. Both the British and the French thought they were right, like when my brothers, sister and I fight! Just like with the Indian people, our little sister only watches because nobody will listen to her. WHAT A MESS! Poor Sir John A. must have been so tired, but happy when he heard that Nova Scotia, New Brunswick, Quebec and Ontario decided to join Canadian Confederation, and become the first four provinces.

All of my Dad's family came from Scotland. All of my mom's relatives (except for one who came from France) were born here, even before, the Europeans started coming over. We're kind of a mixture, but I guess, that's what makes us Canadian. We sure are lucky to have a big family. When we go to our grandparents' houses, we all try to do things the same because we are just so glad to see each other. I think that Sir John A. probably knew, that people would just HAVE to learn, to get along.

NEW BRUNSWICK 1867

THE NAME CHANGES OF CANADA

① 1534   Kanata
           New France

② 1605

③ 1791   Upper Canada
           Lower Canada

④ 1840   Canada East
           Canada West

⑤ 1867 The Provinces of Ontario, Quebec, New Brunswick and Nova Scotia in the Country of Canada

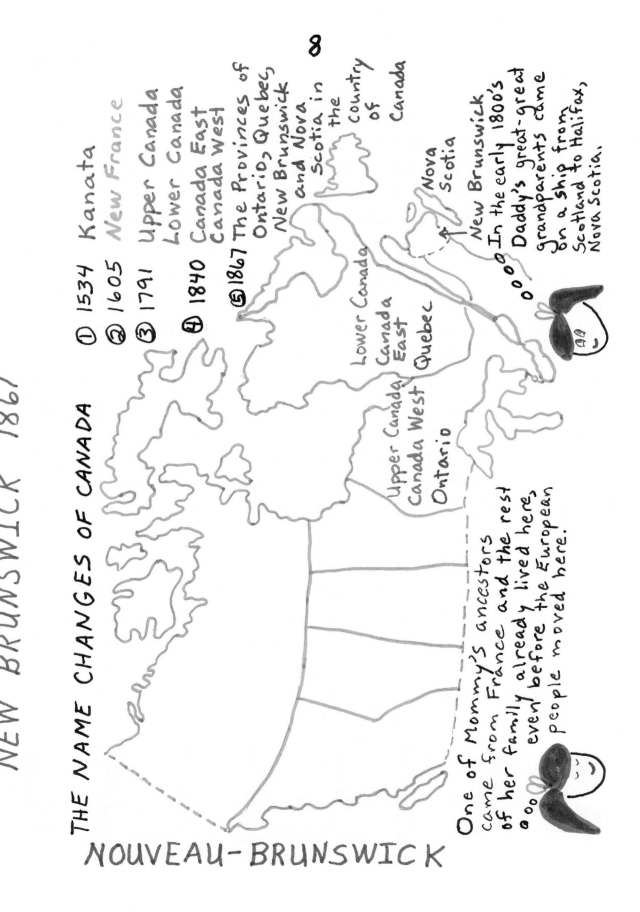

8

Lower Canada
Canada East
Quebec

Upper Canada
Canada West
Ontario

Nova Scotia

New Brunswick. In the early 1800's Daddy's great-great grandparents came on a ship from Scotland to Halifax, Nova Scotia.

One of Mommy's ancestors came from France and the rest of her family already lived here, even before the European people moved here.

NOUVEAU-BRUNSWICK

<u>February 1967</u>

Dear Diary,

Today, Mr. P. showed us a picture of Sir John A. Macdonald and the Fathers of Confederation. There sure were a lot of them! They were all wearing black suits with long black coats and black stovepipe hats, kind of like what Ebenezer Scrooge wore in "A Christmas Carol".

A

It's hard to believe that when my great-grandparents were my age, Canada wasn't even a country yet. Queen Victoria and the government in England made all our laws. I guess if games and schools have to have rules, then towns and countries, have to have laws. A-a-a-anyway, Grandma said both hers and Grandpa's families lived in the part that was once called Upper Canada. Both their parents had farms in Lochiel Township in Glengarry County, Ontario. Since it was such a small place, and Montreal, Quebec was only a few hours away, Grandma's grandmother and aunts used to love to take the train to go shopping there. That was thee-ee-ee-ee place to go, if you wanted to see the latest styles! At one time, Quebec used to be called Lower Canada.

I wonder who made up the names of Upper and Lower Canada? They must have been looking at the map upside down because Quebec looks "more upper" than Ontario does! Maybe tha-a-a-at's why-y-y-y they finally changed the names to Canada East (which became Quebec) and Canada West (which became Ontario).

<u>March 1967</u>

Dear Diary,

Our music teacher taught us a song called "CA-NA-DA" which was written by a man named Bobby Gimby. I think she said that he's from Saskatchewan. In it, he says that there are 20 MILLION people in Canada. *W-w-w-w-ow-ow-ow-ow!*

For our figure skating carnival on March 10th, everyone will wear costumes of allthe different nationalities of people living in our country. I'm going to wear a Scottish kilt, like the ones on the front of the records that Grandpa Campbell plays on the stereo (I know all the words, just like I do for the "Mary Poppins" one that we get to listen to afterwards.). I feel proud listening to the bagpipes like our ancestors played. Donna who just turned 8, will be a French girl like Grandpa Green's great-great-grandmother. Our brother Mark who's 6, is excited because he gets to be a cowboy! Daddy and our 4-year-old brother Danny, will be Confederation Fathers. Laurel our baby sister, will sit in the stands with our mom, grandparents, Aunt Harriet, Uncle Joe and our cousin Ian who's the same age as me. I still have to ask my friend Jayne what she's going to be.

Every night after work, our dad has been busy building stuff for the carnival. Donna and I told all our friends that he made the big wooden Centennial symbol, that hangs over the arena door. When he was working on it, Daddy said that just like the maple leaf on our flag, it has 11 points to represent the 10 provinces and both territories. He still has to finish the huge cake that we'll use in the finale. *It's Daddy's real birthday that night, so I joked and said that he has to make his own cake!* There's going to be a giant *R-R-R-RE-E-E-AL* one, with ICE-CREAM, for all the kids in Ottawa, on July 1st.

NOVA SCOTIA 1867

NOUVELLE-ÉCOSSE

<u>April 1967</u>

Dear Diary,

Grandma and Grandpa Campbell said that they're going to Montreal to see the world's fair in June. Uncle Joe was only 8 in 1930 when his family moved there from Hungary, and my uncle-to-be, Jean-Marie was born near there. Grandpa said that the explorers, fur traders and missionaries all settled in Nova Scotia and along the St. Lawrence River when they first came to Canada.

It's easy to remember the first 2 that got here after the Vikings did, because they have the same initials as I do. John Cabot came in the late 1400's, and Jacques Cartier near the middle of the 1500's. After them, Samuel de Champlain got here in the early 1600's and since he was from France, he called this new place, New France. Jacques Cartier was from France too, but he just used "Kanata", a name that an Indian chief and his braves told him. This is where the name "Canada" came from. It would've been easier if they just used this name from the beginning, instead of changing it so many times! Yesterday I got in trouble, when Donna told on me, for calling her "Donnacona". I don't know what the big deal was, if I was just saying the name of an Indian chief!

The fair is called "Man and His World" or "La Terre Des Hommes" in French, but everyone is calling it "Expo 67". It'll open on April 28th. Grandma said, going there will be like taking a trip around the world, in one stop! Each person will get a souvenir passport that will be stamped in each country's pavilion.

Boy, there sure are a lot of things going on this year! Uncle Ronnie got married to Aunt Jackie in Toronto. It was a nighttime wedding.

ONTARIO 1867

ONTARIO

Uncle Ronnie is the youngest one in Daddy's family. He's the last one to get married since our dad Bill, and mom Anita, got married. Aunt Jackie who moved here from England to work at Expo 67, even wore a white mini-dress. Mommy said that everyone is wearing mini-skirts over there, so now, *e-e-e-everyone* is wearing them here!

<u>May 1967</u>

Dear Diary,

Daddy, Grandpa Campbell, Uncles Joe and Gil and Mr. Langman who is Aunt Doreen's dad, were all jumping up and down and yelling when they watched the Toronto Maple Leafs win the Stanley Cup! Aunt Ruth and Uncle Gil's dog Bonnie got scared and ran into the kitchen to be where Grandma, Aunts Harriet and Ruth, Mommy and Mrs. Langman, were making sandwiches for everyone. One of them said that it was too bad that the Montreal Canadians didn't win, so they could show it off at Expo 67.

My dad and a lot of my friends' fathers, are growing beards just like the ones the Confederation Fathers had. Daddy said, a lot of men had beards in those days because they didn't have sharp razors. I wonder why Sir John A. didn't have a beard.

All the kids at my school have been running and doing special exercises to get Centennial Athlete badges. My friend, Mary B. got a gold. I got a silver, and my other friend, Donna R. got a bronze. Everyone also got a souvenir Confederation dollar. **I-I-I-I'm going to keep mi-i-i-i-ne forever!**

Our new Governor General The Right Honourable Roland Michener loves to run too. I think he's from Alberta. Our old one, Major General Georges Vanier died in March this year. Everybody will miss him. He was from Quebec and he lo-o-o-oved to go to hockey games! Before him, was Vincent Massey, who was the very first one to be born in Canada. **Queen Victoria always had to send Governor Generals over from England to represent her,** because she was so busy taking care of her 9 kids and all her countries. Her great-great granddaughter, **Queen Elizabeth,** who only has 4 kids and can come on a plane, **started picking people who already live here! Maybe it's cheaper!**

QUEBEC 1867

QUÉBEC

MANITOBA 1870

<u>June 1967</u>

Dear Diary,

We've had lots of changes in Canada in the past couple of years. I remember watching on T.V. when we got our new flag called "The Maple Leaf". Grandma said this happened in 1965 and that some Canadians didn't want a new one. They liked having the old one called "The Red Ensign" because it had Britain's flag called "The Union Jack" on it. She said there was a big hoopla because some people wanted to be like the British, and others just wanted to be Canadian. I guess that's why we sing "O Canada" every morning, instead of "God Save the Queen", like we used to. Now we'll only sing it if the queen or Governor General is around. Since our school is called "Queen St. School", they should come to visit us.

Daddy shaved his beard off. He said that it was too hot to have a beard in summertime. When I told him that Mr. S. across the street, still had his, and that you couldn't even see his skin through it, Daddy said that he'd rather be a clean shaven Confederation Father!

Grandma and Grandpa Campbell sent us postcards from Expo 67. They said that Expo was great, except there were too many people and it was too hot. They're coming home on Saturday. That's when Uncle Mackie, Aunt Doreen and their kids Lynne, Grant, Rhonda, Beth and Tracy are coming. They have to drive all the way from St. John, New Brunswick with their camper and their dog Samantha. Uncle Ronnie and Aunt Jackie are coming too. I can't wait!

MANITOBA

July 1967

Dear Diary,

July and December are the BEST months in the *who-o-o-o-le-le-le-le* year! My birthday is on JULY 14th when there's *n-n-n-no-o-o-o* SCHOOL!. Summer School at the park doesn't count though. All we do is arts and crafts, listen to stories, play games and sing songs like "Found A Peanut" or "Who Stole the Cookie From The Cookie Jar?". I love being able to see Kim and Debbie from my old neighbourhood on Elm St.

July 1st is a holiday called Dominion Day. It's called that because we live in the Dominion of Canada, but to me, *it would be easier* just to say Canada Day. Queen Elizabeth, came *a-a-a-a-all the way* over to Ottawa to go to the 100th birthday party. It must have been something to watch it in colour, like on the colour T.V.'s in the store windows. They REALLY cost a lot! Since most people only have black and white ones, it was hard to tell if the queen's purse and shoes matched her dress, like Grandma always says they do.

In Welland, we had a big parade downtown. My best friend Mary W. who lives two doors down from us, wore a long baby blue dress with a petticoat and a matching bonnet, that her mother made. Lots of people wearing Centennial dresses and outfits, rode on decorated bicycles, on horses or in old cars, and lots of the bands played the "CA-NA-DA" song. Everyone knew all the words in both French and English because we've heard Bobby Gimby play it on his trumpet a zillion times. The T.V. and radio people call him "Canada's Pied Piper" because kids from all over Canada got to sing and march with him across football and baseball fields. I wish I could have been one of those kids, like my friend Reg! That song makes me proud of being a Canadian!

NORTHWEST TERRITORIES 1870

TERRITOIRES DU NORD-OUEST

I can't wait to go on our summer holidays! We're leaving in two weeks to go to our other grandparents' place. Maybe we'll go to Expo too, but I can't wait to go and buymy favourite comic books or french fries at the chipstand downtown or go picking berries with our Aunts Judy and Dooners, so they can make pies for us. Sometimes on Sundays, they bring our *who-o-o-o-le-le-le-le* family swimming and barbecuing at Champlain Park. On *re-e-e-e-e-al-al-al-al-al-ly* HOT days, we all go for a midnight swim. It's cooler then, and so we all go down to the river with Mommy, Grandma Green and Aunts Shirley and Rhoda. By the time we walk all the way back up the hill on Sixth St. and have bologna sandwiches and freshie, it's almost 12 o'clock.

L

August 1967

Dear Diary,

Whenever we go on vacation to Grandma and Grandpa Green's, I always like to sing. Since we don't have a radio, it makes the trip go by faster and maybe I won't get carsick!It's 350 miles to drive to Mattawa from our place. Daddy told us that when Mark asked, "How many more miles?" We were barely out of the city so that's why Daddy also said, "And don't keep asking!"

This year the highway was *re-e-e-e-a-a-a-a-lly-y-y-y* busy because *s-s-s-so-o-o-o* many people were driving to Expo. We saw lots of young people hitchhiking. My dad called them "hippies". They were trying to get free rides by holding up signs that said "Expo 67 or Bust". Daddy said that they should get a job instead of singing Beatles songs all day, and trying to get rides. I think that John, Paul, George and Ringo are cute with their funny Beatle haircuts, but now they are letting their hair *gr-r-r-r-row-ow-ow-ow too-oo-oo-oo lo-o-o-o-ng!*

We saw lots of old cars like Model T Fords coming from places like Alberta, Manitoba, the Yukon and Northwest Territories. Everyone was using the Trans Canada Highway that goes from British Columbia to Newfoundland. When we tried to see who could read a licence plate from the furthest place first, our dad or I, always won. Donna said, *"That's no fair because you guys are sitting in the front, so you get to see them first!"* Whenever we saw a car coming, Danny and Laurel would yell *"There's one, there's one!"* even though they can't even read. When we saw a car from P.E.I. heading out west, Mommy said "Hey, they're going the wrong way!"

BRITISH COLUMBIA 1871

COLOMBIE-BRITANNIQUE

<u>September 1967</u>

Dear Diary,

I'm so happy that I get Mr. P. again because he's teaching grade 5 too. *He-e-e-e's* my favourite teacher! It seemed like most of the kids in my class went to Expo this summer, or knew someone who did. When Mr. P. asked who went, I put my hand up too.

Mommy and Daddy went to Expo, so we almost went. Since we had so much fun last summer, we all wanted to stay at Aunt Honey's (her real name is Elizabeth, but Grandpa Campbell always called her "Honey") and Uncle Ken's again, with their kids Paul, Joel, Kenny and Liza in Petawawa, Ontario. Our cousin Ian was there too, with his parents and his dog Shoo-Shoo (Aunt Honey's cats weren't very happy!). We all went to stay at a cottage on a lake. Our mom said that it wasn't too far from the Golden Lake Reserve, where her grandmother Maggie, was born. Our dad said that we were lucky, because it was *a-a-a-a-a-l-l-l-l-o-o-o-o-t coo-oo-oo-ooler* at the beach, than being in Montreal. I told him, it was, except that the sand was so HOT, you could hardly walk on it!

For Current Events Time at school, almost everyone brought souvenirs that had the Expo 67 or Centennial symbol on it. I-I-I-I brought in, an embroidered pillow that had a map of Canada and the dates, when each province or territory joined Canada on it. Even if I didn't go to Expo 67, I still feel like I did! I got to see the little Centennial Train museum that was traveling across Canada and I went with the school choir to the spring festival, and sang the song about Ontario that was in the Ontario pavilion at Expo!

ÎLE-DU-PRINCE-ÉDOUARD

October 1967

Dear Diary,

    October is my *thir-r-r-rd* favourite month because I love seeing pictures of jack-o-lanterns, and witches flying with black cats on broomsticks, across the moon. This Halloween was *th-e-e-e-* BEST, because we went to our first Halloween party at Mary's house. It was just like the one in "It's the Great Pumpkin Charlie Brown". Mary's older sisters gave out prizes and her brother played records. We got some Centennial money and chocolate bars. Donna and I couldn't tell Mark, Danny and Laurel because it was only for big kids.

    Expo closed yesterday on October 28th. Millions of people from all over the world went to see it. Grandma said that we lived through a piece of history, just like her parents did 100 years ago, when Queen Victoria and the British Parliament passed the British North American Act (B.N.A. Act) that made Canada into a country with its own government. They probably saw the picture in the newspapers of the Confederation Fathers having meetings in Charlottetown, Prince Edward Island. I should ask Mr. P. why-y-y-y they had the meetings there, because the people in P.E.I. didn't even want to join Canada yet! Sure glad they did, because that's where "Anne of Green Gables" lived. Someday, *I-I-I-I'd* like to go there and visit.

Since there were only 4 provinces in Canada on July 1st 1867, Sir John A. Macdonald had to do *som-m-m-m-mething* to get the other colonies to join. One important thing was to build a railroad *ri-i-i-i-ight* across Canada. When everybody heard about this, they were EXCITED because it would be a lot faster to go by train, than by stagecoach or horse and wagon. Grandma's dad, Great-Grandpa MacLeod and his five brothers helped to build that railroad. Every spring they would go away to work on it, then come back in the fall, buy another piece of farmland and build a house on it. Pretty soon they all had their own homes when they got married.

Soon the other colonies joined Canada, all except Newfoundland that waited until 1949. It was kind of like when my family plays Monopoly. Daddy says *"If you want-to-get-any-money-from-the-bank, you have to join in on the game"* and *"There's NO CRYING, if you have to give it back!"*.

ALBERTA 1905

ALBERTA

<u>November 1967</u>

Dear Diary,

Centennial Year is almost finished and I feel sad, kind of like when my cousin Ian's grandmother died this summer.

We had *a-a-a-a-nother* wedding in our family this year. Aunt Dooners whose real name "Teresa", means "Little Flower", got married to Uncle Jean-Marie in August. Grandpa Green, who has worked for more than 50 summers as a fishing guide at a camp on Lake Temagami, even flew home for the weekend. Now, both of Mommy's youngest sisters are married because Aunt Judy who *I-I-I-I'm* named after, got married two Christmases ago to Uncle Romeo. Uncle Biddy whose real name is Robert, played at both of their weddings. Everyone loves to watch him play the mandolin, guitar or violin because he plays by ear, and makes it look so easy. He's Grandma Green's o-o-o-only boy, and that's why she calls him *"My Son, Moon and Stars"*!

Everyone except my mom lives in Mattawa. It's a little town along the Ottawa and Mattawa Rivers. Mattawa is an Algonquin word that means "Meeting of the Waters". If you look across the Ottawa River on the Quebec side, you can see the Laurentian Mountains. There are 3 white crosses up there. Whenever I see them, I *a-a-a-a-l-l-l-l-l-wa-a-a-a-ys* wonder, if the French and Scottish explorers would look up at them when they were paddling down the Ottawa, and then the Mattawa, on their way out west.

8

Although Mommy and Daddy were born in different places and come from different backgrounds, they both lived along or near the Ottawa River. Even when they grew up, they both went to work in Deep River which is a little place, somewhere in between theirhometowns.. That's why, when I'm listening to my teacher talk about the days of the explorers, *I-I-I-I* feel like, *I'm studying my family's history too.*

December 1967

Dear Diary,

For Christmas we got lots of presents like board games, puzzles, paint-by-number sets, skates, barbies, race cars, clothes and books. I got a 'Tom Sawyer" book just like the one that Mr. P. read to us, at the end of every school day. Too bad it couldn't be Christmas all year! I love all the Christmas stories, singing Christmas Carols, putting up decorations, watching all the Christmas shows and movies and most of all going to Grandma and Grandpa's for a turkey dinner with all our family!

Grandma said that she heard on the news that Bobby Gimby will become a memberof the Order of Canada. I'm so glad that I bought the 45 record with his song "CA-NA-DA", so I can play it for *m-m-m m -y* grandchildren one day.

I will never forget this year especially because I had two birthdays in July. On July 1ˢᵗ, I turned 100 and on my real birthday, I turned 10. *Does that make me 110 this year?*

What about my cousins Patrick and Cheryl who were born last year? Or what about Sean, Michael, Robbie and Katelyn and my other cousins? My newest, little cousin Jamie, was born just this morning, on the very last day of Centennial Year. *Does that make him 100 years old today too?*

Stan Skyler Tara Terry Timmy Tina Toby Tommy

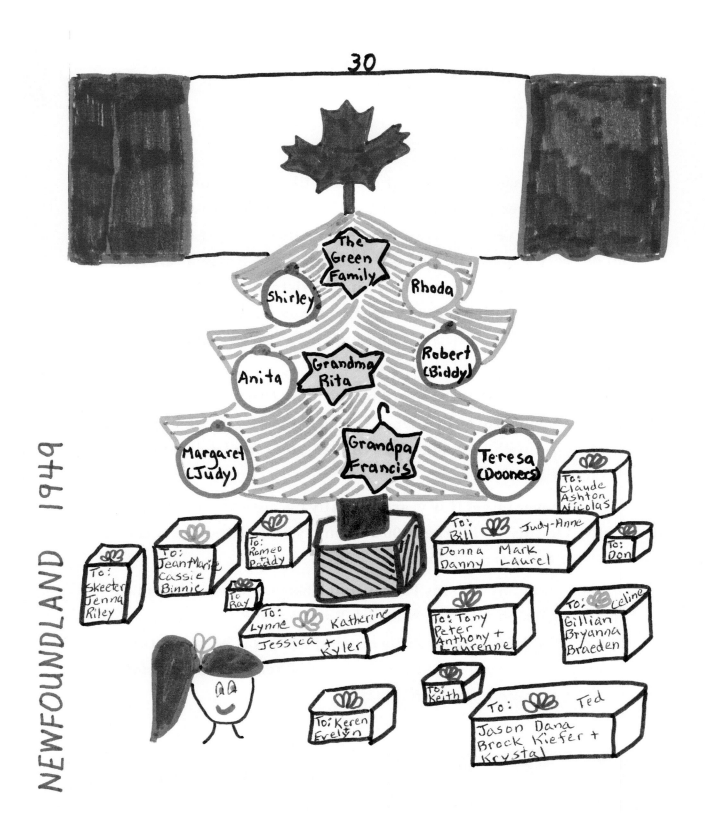

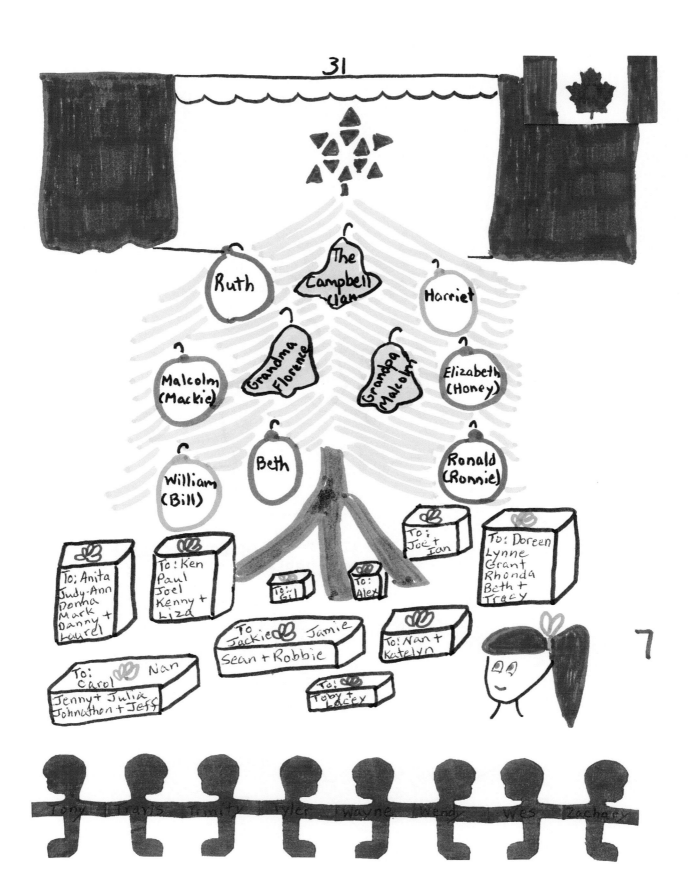

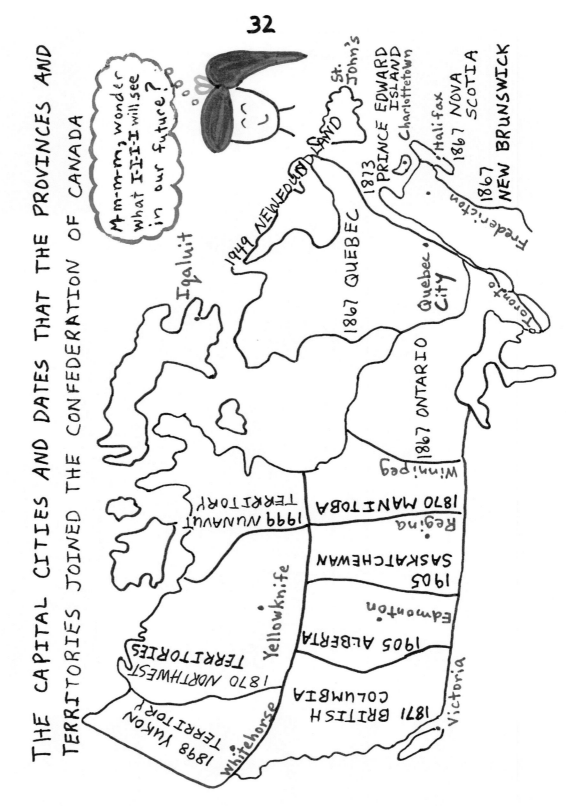

NUNAVUT 1999

THE CAPITAL CITIES AND DATES THAT THE PROVINCES AND TERRITORIES JOINED THE CONFEDERATION OF CANADA

NUNAVUT

Printed in the United States
by Baker & Taylor Publisher Services